Islam 101

Reaching Out With Understanding

Islam 101

Reaching Out With Understanding

Lorraine Orris

*Life*CONNEXIONS

Win...Build...Send...people for Christ

ACKNOWLEDGEMENTS

I would like to thank my husband David for encouraging me, and believing in me throughout the writing of this book. I am also deeply grateful for the spiritual insight and literary contributions of two fine men affiliated with Campus Crusade for Christ.

Islam 101: Reaching Out With Understanding
© 2004 Lorraine Orris

New Life Publications
A Ministry of Campus Crusade for Christ
375 Highway 74 South, Suite A
Peachtree City, GA 30269

Designed by The LegacyRoad Group
Edited by The LegacyRoad Group
First Printing, 2004
Printed in the United States of America
ISBN 1-56399-217-5

Library of Congress Cataloging-in-Publication Data
CIP applied for

TABLE OF CONTENTS

INTRODUCTION

With intense, ongoing turmoil in the Middle East, it is of utmost importance that Christians gain a basic knowledge and understanding of Islam and the Muslim worldview.

I was prompted to write this book because of a friendship I share with a Muslim woman. Relationships build slowly in the Muslim culture but are highly valued and long-lasting. Many times this dear friend has said that she will be my friend forever. While she and I have little in common, her steadfast loyalty is genuine, consistent, and rich. I value her and her friendship greatly.

As her friend, I care about the misconceptions the

Muslim world has about God's Word and the Christian faith. I am also concerned about the spiritual bondage that enslaves billions of precious souls around the world.

Together, these realities have given me a deep and abiding respect and concern for Muslim people for whom Jesus died on the cross. Many Christians despair at the prospect of individuals from Islamic traditions or cultures ever finding faith in Christ. But as the testimonies at the end of this volume attest, Muslims are finding their way to faith in Him. Recent trends seem to be indicating that for the first time there is not only an openness to hearing the Gospel, but also a new responsiveness to it.

This is a basic, informational book intended as an introductory educational resource for the Christian world. It is important to know the facts of this fast-growing religion in order to relate to Muslims and better reach them with the Good News of Christ. After a brief look at Islam and Muhammad, we will examine in greater detail the major elements of Islam. We will then offer some tips on sharing your faith with Muslims. Finally, we will share some real-life testimonies of former Muslims who have become Christians.

We hope and pray this little book will help you...

• See the opportunities of ministry to Muslims in your world today.

• Clearly understand the principle facts regarding

Islam.

• Become motivated and prepared to share what Christ has done for you.

• Feel compassion and concern for the deep and real spiritual needs of the millions of magnificent people who live under the influence of Islam.

We have written this book in a simple and straight-forward manner. As you read it, please ask God to give you a passion for sharing Christ's love and Good News with Muslim people through patience, kindness, and clarity.

Understanding Islam

ISLAM IN BRIEF

I slam was founded by the prophet Muhammad in Arabia (modern-day Saudi Arabia) in the early seventh century. This period in Arabia, before Islam's birth, is referred to as the "time of arrogance." The people of that area were largely polytheistic and idolatrous. Muhammad was concerned about the various forms of religion at that time and would often go to the hills to meditate. It was during this time that he claimed to have been visited by the angel Gabriel who brought messages from Allah.

Muhammad's first converts consisted mostly of family members in Mecca. Most of the inhabitants of Mecca rejected Muhammad's teaching, accusing him of being demon-possessed. As the opposition to Muhammad's teaching intensified, he and his followers, about fifty at that time, made the move from Mecca to the city of Medina. While in Medina, Islam began to take on a clearer doctrine. Muhammad became a statesman, a legislator, and a judge. His converts grew as his influence increased, and large-scale warfare became widespread. In just eight years, the Muslim armies succeeded in changing the Arab-speaking world from polytheistic to mainly Muslim.

Today, Islam is one of the fastest-growing religions in the United States. By the year 2010 America's Muslim population is expected to surpass the Jewish population, making Islam the country's second-largest faith after Christianity.

There are a little over 1,200 mosques in the U.S., as well as numerous Islamic day schools, and weekend schools.

Though Islam was once largely confined to Arabia and parts of Africa, it has now spread from spiritual centers such as this "forbidden city" (North Africa) and into rural America.

BIOGRAPHY OF MUHAMMAD

According to various Islamic sources, the story of Muhammad's life was passed on from generation to generation, through the telling of stories. His story begins with his birth in the sixth century. The son of Amina and Abdulla Muttalib, he was born in the city of Mecca, in Arabia. His father died before he was born, so at the time of his birth, his mother, Amina, sent for his grandfather, her father. His grandfather came and took him to the Ka'bah, the ancient temple in Mecca where he prayed for the infant and gave him the name of Muhammad.

It was customary in those days to hire a nursing mother from the Arabian desert to take the child and nurse him for the first two years, so the child would have the benefit of the clean, fresh air of the desert, rather than the cramped, contaminating air of the city.

A woman named Halima, from the tribe of Bani S'ad, had come to the city of Mecca in search of a child who needed a nurse. This was her means of employment, but neither she nor the other women who had come seeking nursing babies wanted to nurse Muhammad because his father was dead. They didn't think they would be well paid. But, suddenly, after Halima had refused Amina, she had an overwhelming desire for the child. So, she then took Muhammad to her Bedouin home. Immediately, her breasts overflowed with milk, and the udders of her female camel also were full. Everything about her seemed to flourish. The women of the tribe became envious of her because of her great luck, and they spread rumors that she had a blessed child.

When Muhammad was two years old, Halima brought him back to his mother. However, because he had brought her so much luck, she begged her to let her keep him a while longer. Amina agreed.

It is taught that one day, when the child Muhammad was out alone, two angels came and seized him, opened up his chest, and took out his heart. They removed a small, black stone, cleaned the cavity, and put the heart back. Thus, a "devil" was removed from him, and he was made "pure."

As a small child he tended the goats with his foster brothers and learned the pure, Arabic language of the Bedouins. When he was six and back with his mother, she took him to Yathnib to pay a visit to her father. She also wanted to visit the grave of her husband. On her way back to Mecca, she became suddenly ill, and died at a place called Abwa. An Abyssinian woman named Umm Ayman Barkah found and brought the child to his grandfather in Mecca. He became the apple of his grandfather's eye.

At the age of eight, Muhammad's grandfather died. After that he was cared for by two uncles. Once, when he was nine, his Uncle Abu Talib planned to go with a merchant caravan to Syria. The child begged to go with him and his uncle finally agreed. When the caravan reached Busra, in Syria, the group broke for a short stay. While there, a monk who was meditating in a nearby cave saw the child and received a revelation that the child was special. He went to the boy's uncle and told him that Muhammad had the "signs" of a future prophet, and that he should take him back home right away. He also told him to guard the child carefully, especially from the Jews. So, Abu Talib returned to Mecca with the child.

Muhammad grew to be a reserved, honest, and unassuming young man. While others his age were behaving boisterously and discovering the ways of evil, Muhammad worked hard as a shepherd and goat herder.

According to one story, when Muhammad was about fourteen or fifteen, a war broke out between his tribe, the Qu'raysh, and another, the Hawazin. After a volley of arrows had been shot, Muhammad picked up the enemies' arrows and offered them back.

At the age of twenty-five, Muhammad married his first wife, Khadijah. She was fifteen years his elder, a widow, and a brilliant and wealthy business woman. She was honest and very well respected. Muhammad had seven children with Khadijah, although not all of them lived.

When Muhammad was thirty-five, a reconstruction of the Ka'bah began. At that time, the Ka'bah was the home of all sorts of statues and idols of pagan gods. After the building had begun reconstruction, there was much fighting and arguing between the different tribes about who should place the holy, black stone in its place. There was so much fighting that the construction stopped. Then they decided that the first man entering the building in the morning would be the one to place the stone in its place. The first man turned out to be Muhammad. Instead of placing the black stone by himself, he took a large, sturdy cloth, placed the stone in the middle of it, and had each of the different tribes take an end. They all put the stone in place together. Thus began his reputation for wisdom.

As the story goes, in the year A.D. 610 Muhammad received his religious call; he was about forty. When he received his first revelation, he was terrified that it had come from demons, or Jinn, as the Muslims call them. But his wife assured him that the revelation was from God, or Allah, as that was the name that was revealed to him. (There had been an "Allah" prior to this time, who was a god of the pre-Muslim pantheon.)

Muhammad's teachings were not well received in Mecca, so in June of 622 he journeyed to make his home in Medina. This event marked the beginning of the Islamic calendar. Eight years later, Muhammad returned to Mecca in triumph for he had gained many followers and converts to Islam. He felt that the "gods" in the Ka'bah were evil, so he went to the Ka'bah and purified it by removing the various idols in the ancient Arab shrine.

It is said that Muhammad continued to receive revelations, and by the time of his death two years later all of Arabia was committed to Islam.

Understanding Islam

FREQUENTLY ASKED QUESTIONS ABOUT ISLAM

1. What is Islam?

It is the teaching of the prophet Muhammad, and in practice is a combination of religion, culture, and sometimes politics. It is the official state religion of many Muslim countries.

2. What does "Islam" mean?

It means "Submission to the will of Allah."

3. Do Muslims believe that theirs is the only true religion?

They believe that their religion is above all others because the revelation to Muhammad was the last and final one, and therefore the most accurate.

4. What does "Allah" mean?

It means: "The Supreme Being." It is the name of God, possibly derived from the Arabic word Al-Ilah, "the one who is exalted."

5. What are the differences between God and Allah?

The God of the Bible is righteous. He is our Father in Heaven, a triune God. He evokes thoughts of love, compassion, tenderness, protectiveness, and grace. God sacrificed His own Son for the eternal salvation of sinners. "For by grace are you saved." Christianity was founded by a risen Savior.

Allah is the creator and judge. He is a god of power. He demands total submission and obedience. He created both good and evil. He predetermined all things which happen in the world. Therefore, if something bad happens, it is the will of Allah.

Allah has done nothing for man that has cost him anything. One's salvation is achieved through works. Where Christianity was founded by a risen Savior, Islam was founded by a now deceased prophet.

6. Is Islam a peaceful religion?

Muhammad gained followers by using force. He had converts who were warriors and would invade villages, take physical control, and demand that the captives become Muslim. This is the way in which Islam was spread throughout Arabia. To reject Allah and Islam was to invite death.

The Qur'an states, "Fight and slay the pagans (anyone not Muslim) wherever ye find them, and lie in wait for them in every stratagem of war…" (Surah 9:5). "Fight those who do not believe in God and the last day… and fight the people of the book (Jews and Christians) who do not accept the religion of truth (Islam) …" (Surah 9:29). "I will instill terror into the hearts of unbelievers, smite ye above their necks and smite all their fingertips off them" (Surah 8:13-17). In dozens of places in the Qur'an, Allah promises Paradise to anyone who is martyred when killing the "infidels of God." That is as close to assurance of salvation as Islam gives. As an aside, today in Israel and other Middle Eastern countries, when a Muslim becomes a suicide bomber, his or her family is generously, financially compensated. Yet some can find interpretations that contradict these Surahs to show that Islam might be a peaceful religion.

7. What are the five laws or pillars of Islam?

They are: (1.) Confession that there is no God but Allah and that Muhammad is his prophet or; (2.) Prayer, five times each day; (3.) Charitable giving to the poor; (4.) Fasting during the holy month of Ramadan; and (5.) The hajj, a pilgrimage to Mecca for those who are able.

8. How often do Muslims pray?

Muslims pray 5 times a day, before sunrise, at noon, in the early afternoon, at sundown, and at night. Specific timing is determined by local clerics and may vary from one location to another.

9. What makes Mecca a holy place?

It is the place of the miracle of the black stone, and the place of Muhammad's birth.

10. Do American Muslims believe that Usama Bin Laden is evil?

"Maybe. Maybe not. He is just a man," says one American Muslim. Some believe there is no proof that he was the mastermind behind the attacks of September 11, 2001, on the World Trade Center and the Pentagon. Some feel that the American news media is biased and tries to make people believe what it wants. The same is true of opinions of Saddam Hussein, the Taliban of Afghanistan, and other world figures.

11. Did people believe in Allah before Muhammad or the Qur'an?

Yes and No. There was a god named Allah who was one of three chief idols of the pre-Islamic pantheon worshiped at the Ka'bah which consisted of 360 idols. Muhammad's revelation was that Al-lah, whom he already knew, was the one true God.

12. How many wives did Muhammad have?

Most accounts say that Muhammad had fifteen wives, though a few accounts say that he had only twelve. Others say Muhammad had four wives. There is really no terribly accurate account of his marriages. The account which says he had four wives says that his first was forty years old when he was twenty-five. His second wife was about eighteen years old. His third was a Christian. His fourth was about ten years old when they married. It is taught that he had these various kinds of wives in order to show his followers what sorts of wives Muslim men could have. They could be older, widowed, younger, very much younger, or of different faiths. Men were allowed to marry up to four wives, as long as they treated each equally and showed no favoritism. Women, on the other hand, could only marry one man.

QUESTIONS ABOUT THE QUR'AN

13. What are the holy books of Islam?

The Qur'an is the only accepted holy book of Islam. Other books, The Torah of Moses, The Psalms of David, and The Gospel of Jesus Christ, are believed to have once had authoritative status, but were corrupted over the years. Muslims believe the Qur'an is God's most recent, most accurate, and final word to man. Muslims also believe that many other books were given to other prophets, but they have all been lost or corrupted beyond recognition.

14. What is the Qur'an?

This is the authoritative scripture of Islam. It is about two-thirds the size of the New Testament. Divided into one hundred fourteen Surahs, or chapters, it is an extensive guide for Muslim believers.

15. Did Muhammad write the Qur'an?

Muhammad claimed to have received the teachings of the Qur'an in revelations from Allah via the angel Gabriel, from age 40 until his death. The Qur'an was not put down in writing until after his death. Muhammad could neither read nor write.

16. What are the major teachings of the Qur'an?

It teaches that Allah is one being. It teaches Muslim followers to pray five times a day and to worship by reciting the Qur'an. It teaches predestination, the five laws to which followers should absolutely submit, and it gives detailed instructions on what to say in prayers and how to live.

QUESTIONS ABOUT ISLAMIC TERMS

17. What is the black stone?

The story goes that a big, black stone fell from the heavens to the Arabian desert (probably a meteorite).

Because it came from the sky, the people thought it was from God and began to believe that the place on which it fell was holy. (Later, that place became known as Mecca.) After Ishmael was born to Sarah's servant, Hagar, Sarah was very jealous and hated Hagar. Sarah demanded that Abraham get rid of her. So, Abraham took Hagar and her child into the desert and left them there. (See Geneiss v. 21.) Hagar walked and walked until she thought she would die of thirst. She sat down and started digging and digging for water, and miraculously found water right where the black stone had fallen. Today, the stone is in a wall of the Ka'bah, in Mecca, Saudi Arabia.

18. What is Ramadan?

Ramadan is a Muslim calendar month when Muslims celebrate Allah's giving of the Qur'an to Muhammad. It is a time for celebration, fasting, and prayer. And, it is at a different time each year. It follows a Muslim lunar calendar and is ten days later each year than the year before.

19. What is *jihad?*

The word *jihad* is frequently misunderstood by both Christians and Muslims. The word means, simply, "struggle." It is sometimes referred to as the "sixth pillar" of Islam due to its importance, but this is misleading: in Islam, there are two forms of *jihad*. The Lesser *jihad* is "the *jihad* of the sword," or use of personal or military force, and is commanded and permissible only when Muslims are oppressed and prohibited from worshiping freely. Many Muslims and most non-Muslims perceive this as the only form of *jihad,* and extremist Muslim interpretations of oppression further the misunderstanding. The Greater *jihad* is "the *jihad* of the heart," a personal struggle for righteousness commanded of all Muslims at all times.

Understanding Islam

A DIALOGUE: COMPARING MUSLIM AND CHRISTIAN BELIEFS

In reaching out to those of the Islamic faith, it is important for Christians to know what Muslims believe about Christianity. The following dialogue is designed to show how Muslims view important elements of the Christian faith. It is not meant to generalize what every Muslim necessarily believes, but is a sampling of one Muslim's view.

1. WAS JESUS BORN OF A VIRGIN?

Muslim — Yes. His mother was Mary, a virgin. An angel performed a miracle in order that she might conceive. He didn't have a father.

Christian – Yes. His mother was Mary. His Father was God.

2. IS JESUS THE SON OF GOD?

Muslim – No. He had no father. God does not have sons, daughters, or intimate partners.

Christian – Yes, but the relationship is a spiritual one, not physical, for He was born of the Holy Spirit of God through the Virgin Mary.

3. DO MUSLIMS BELIEVE IN JESUS?

Muslim – Yes. He was a great prophet and worker of miracles. But, Muslims do not believe in Jesus in the sense of having faith in Him.

Christian – Muslims believe Jesus was a great prophet, but that He was not God or the Son of God.

4. HOW DO YOU GET TO HEAVEN?

Muslim – We get to Heaven, or Paradise, by believing in and serving Allah. We must pray five times each day, and we must do good to others. Still, there is no absolute guarantee. It is up to the will of Allah.

Christian – We must believe that Jesus is the Son of God, and that He died on the cross for our sins; and we must confess our sins, ask to be forgiven, and give our hearts to Him. By grace we are saved through faith, not by works—salvation is the gift of God.

5. WHO IS GREATER, ISAAC OR ISHMAEL?

Muslim – Ishmael is the greatest because he was the first-born of Abraham and Hagar, and is the father of the Arab nation. Abraham too became a Muslim.

Christian – Isaac is greater, because he is the one God designated to be Abraham's heir. Ishmael was the illegitimate child of Hagar, who was urged to conceive a child, by Sarah, Abraham's wife. Sarah's urging came from her disbelief in God's promise to give her and Abraham a miracle child.

6. DID JESUS RISE FROM THE DEAD?

Muslim – No, because He did not die on the cross. God rescued Him some way. He either kept Him alive by allowing Him to "look dead," or by having His followers switch bodies. It was a conspiracy. The people that saw Him alive afterwards either saw the "still alive" Jesus, or were hallucinating.

Christian – Absolutely. Jesus was beaten and tortured

and condemned to death by Romans who were expert executioners. He died on the cross taking the punishment for our sins upon Himself in order to give us eternal life. Also, there are many historical, non-biblical writings which show the crucifixion to be true.

Additional support for the biblical account comes from the cultural circumstances of the spreading of the news. In first-century Jewish culture, women were not highly esteemed. So, the fact that the first people to see Jesus alive after His burial in the tomb were women, according to Matthew 28, Mark 16, Luke 24, and John 20, strongly argues that this is an accurate account. Jesus' followers would have been embarrassed to record this fact, had it not been true.

Also, Jesus was buried in a tomb belonging to a well-respected Jewish leader. That also is unusual, since He was not wealthy or from a prominent family. If Jesus had really been a blasphemer, then a respectable Jewish leader wouldn't have wanted to give Him such a burial.

7. Is Allah a God of love?

Muslim —Yes. He loves us if we do his will. However, the Qur'an says, "God loves not sinners." Allah requires his followers to be good, to do good works, and then he will allow people to go to Heaven.

Christian — Yes. The Christian God loves us while we

are still sinners, and loved us so much that He gave His only son to die for us so that we would not have to pay the penalty for our sins.

8. DO YOU BELIEVE IN THE TRINITY?

Muslim – No. There is no God but Allah. It is not possible to love a God the Father, God the Son, and God the Holy Spirit all the same. Besides, how can one love a God who kills His own son? The trinity is totally illogical.

Christian – Yes. I believe in the Father, the Son, and the Holy Spirit, three persons in one being. The Father sends the Son to earth, the Son is the one who takes on a human nature and becomes incarnate, and the Holy Spirit stands in Christ's place until the Son returns. The Bible, in John 1:1-2, says, "In the beginning was the Word and the Word was with God and the Word was God." Jesus is the Word. Jesus himself refers to the Holy Spirit as separate from Father and Son, but present in the believer (John 14:16-17), and says that this means He (Jesus) is also in the believer (verse 20). See also Luke 12:10.

9. IF YOU DIED TODAY, WOULD YOU GO TO HEAVEN?

Muslim – I cannot answer that. I would be showing arrogance if I said I was sure I would. I would hope I would go to Heaven, but it is up to Allah. Only He knows. Perhaps I will go to Hell first, and then to Heaven. I trust in Allah but do not trust in myself. (Many American Muslims call Allah "God.")

Christian – Absolutely. I have given my life to Christ. I have received Him into my heart and have faith in Him. He has forgiven me and washed away my sins. Yes, I would definitely go to Heaven, not because I am worthy, but because of Christ's love and work on the cross for me.

10. WHAT DO YOU THINK OF JESUS?

Muslim – Jesus was a great and holy prophet who performed many miracles.

Christian – Jesus is the Son of God. He is my savior and Lord.

Reaching Out With Love

PREPARING TO SHARE

Since you now know the basics of Islam, we can proceed to the next practical step: how do you reach a Muslim for Christ? You may also be asking, "How is sharing my faith with a Muslim different from sharing with anyone else?" The message is not different. The method is different. We are all sinners in need of the saving grace that only Christ can provide. But there are some key points that you should know about adherents to Islam. In this section, we will guide you through these points, then give you some final words about witnessing to a Muslim.

First of all, there are three prerequisites for anyone witnessing to Muslims.

1. You must be filled with the Holy Spirit. Jesus said

in John 15:26, "When the Helper comes, whom I will send to you from the Father, that is the Spirit of Truth, who proceeds from the Father, He will bear witness of me." Always remember that when you are sharing with a Muslim you are engaged in an intense spiritual battle. If you are not filled with the Spirit of the Lord, you will find yourself quickly exhausted both spiritually and emotionally. The Holy Spirit will give you wisdom, power, and physical strength and endurance. You do not want to go into battle without Him.

2. You must be in prayer at all times. You will have to pray the Muslim into the Kingdom of God, otherwise you shouldn't even begin to share with him. Islam is based on one presupposition: that Christianity is false. The Muslim claims that Islam exists because Christianity was corrupted, and if ever they accepted Christianity to be true, then Islam would have no reason to exist. Muslims can be very difficult to witness to. At times you will become extremely frustrated and even aggravated. It is at precisely that moment that you should pray, and continue to be in prayer. "Be joyful always; pray continually; give thanks in all circumstances, for this is God's will for you in Christ Jesus." 1 Thess. 5:16-18. "And pray in the Spirit on all occasions with all kinds of prayers and requests." Ephesians 6:18. You cannot enter into an evangelistic appointment of this nature unless you are filled with the Spirit and bathed in prayer.

3. You must have love. Don't look at Muslims with the world's stereotypical eyes, like they are the "fanatic Muslim terrorist." Are over a billion of the world's people terrorists? We need to combat that misconception and see them as those lost without Christ. And, we need to love deeply, sincerely, and steadfastly. Only love will keep us from losing heart when a Muslim rejects Christ. Without love, it is easy to stop praying for him, or to lose interest in spending time with him. "Jesus replied, 'Love the Lord your God with all your heart and with all your soul and with all your mind. This is the first and greatest commandment. And the second is like it: Love your neighbor as yourself. All the Law and the Prophets hang on these two commandments.'" Matthew 22:37-40.

SHARING YOUR FAITH

Five Areas You Need To Explain to a Muslim

There are five major issues which must first be explained and worked through with a Muslim before you will be able to go back and say, "Here is how you can become a Christian":

1. **The authenticity of the Bible**
2. **The consistency of God's revelation**
3. **Why Christians believe Jesus is the Son of God**
4. **Did Jesus really die on the cross?**
5. **The Trinity**

Take the necessary time to explain each of these issues. One Christian worked with a Muslim for a period of over two years. On many occasions they would have all-day meetings, from morning until evening, discussing these things. There *will* be times when you think you're not getting across to your contact; however, this is not true.

As someone once said, "It is not strange for a Muslim to hear the Gospel more than fifty times before it starts to make sense to him." On the other hand, it is not *how many* times you share the truth but *how* you share it that is important. Let us, therefore, discuss in detail each of the above issues.

1. THE AUTHENTICITY OF THE BIBLE*

The Muslims claim that both the Old and New Testaments have been changed, and that the Bible is therefore not trustworthy. For this reason they believe it was necessary for God to give another book, the Qur'an, to replace it. They believe that the Qur'an contains the essence of all the heavenly books, including the Old and New Testaments.

* One good habit to form is always to take your Bible with you and allow the person to read the passage for himself. God's Word is living and active and will minister to him directly. While you may not always have your Bible with you when witnessing opportunities arise, make sure you bring it when meeting again for a Bible study or a follow-up meeting.

A. Can the Word of God really be changed?

In addressing this issue, it is important to direct the

Muslim's attention to the fact that the Bible is God's Word. The following are a few good questions you might consider asking your Muslim friend:

(If the Bible is God's Word, how could man change it?

(Isn't God able to protect His Word from being changed?

(Since the Bible is God's Word, whom are we accusing when we say it's been changed? Aren't we accusing God Himself by saying that He was not able to protect it from being changed?

(Who changed the Bible? When was it changed?

(Which parts were changed? And for what reason?

By asking him such questions, you will soon find out that he does not have answers to any of them. The Muslim simply says, "It was changed," and usually has no proof or evidence to support his allegations.

B. What does the Bible say regarding itself?

Because the Muslim agrees that the Bible is God's Word, you may also want to direct his attention to what it says about itself:

Matthew 5:18: (Christ speaking) "...until heaven and earth disappear, not the smallest letter, not the least stroke of a pen, will by any means disappear from the Law until everything is accomplished."

Matthew 24:35: (Christ speaking) "Heaven and earth will pass away, but my Word will not pass away."

41

1 Peter 1:24, 25: "...the grass withers and the flowers fall off, but the Word of the Lord abides forever." (also Isaiah 40:8)

2 Timothy 3:16: "All scripture is inspired by God and profitable for teaching, for reproof, for correction, and for training in righteousness."

2 Peter 1:21: "For no prophecy was ever made by an act of human will, but men moved by the Holy Spirit spoke from God."

C. What does the Qur'an say about the Bible?

The Qur'an itself does not say the Bible has been changed. In fact, it says that unless one obeys the Torah and the Bible, they are nothing. It mentions the Torah and the "Zabur" (the Old Testament with the Psalms) and the "Injil" (which is the New Testament) many times. When the Qur'an was written, no mention was made of the Bible having been changed. Thus, when Islam began in the sixth century, 600 years after Jesus Christ, the Bible was accepted as true.

D. What about the issue of translation?

The Bible we have in our hands today was translated from the original languages of Hebrew and Greek. Whether it was printed in 1999, 1970, or 1950 it was translated from the original language. There is a complete Bible that dates back to the third century, 300 years after Christ and 400 years before Islam. It is a complete, original

Bible and there are several of these in existence: one in a museum in London and another in the Vatican in Rome.

However, someone may say, "Well, maybe it was changed before the year 300." We have thousands of original copies of various sections of the Bible that date back to before the year 300. If these pieces were put together, the result would be hundreds, if not thousands of complete Bibles dating back to before the year 300. The oldest of these manuscripts dates to around the year A.D. 100. We also know that the first books of the New Testament were written in A.D. 40 or 50. Evidence of this may be found in the writings of the Church Fathers, by whom many books and articles were written prior to A.D. 100. The entire New Testament, with the exception of five sentences that have nothing to do with theology or doctrine, can be reconstructed from the quotes of the church fathers found in these writings. In essence, there are original copies from the same time as the writings of the Apostles who wrote by the inspiration of the Holy Spirit.

E. Why are there four Gospels rather than just one?

Some Muslims argue that Islam has one Qur'an, while Christianity has four Bibles. It is important to explain to them that this is not true. While we have what we call the four Gospels of Matthew, Mark, Luke, and John, these are not divergent accounts but rather the same story told from four different points of view. These four agree on the basics of the life and teachings of Jesus Christ, and none contradicts another. They do not record the entirety of the events surrounding the life of Jesus, but together with the Old and New Testament writings, they combine to form one Bible, inspired by the Holy Spirit. What is interesting is that in the days of Christ, the region of the Middle East where Christ was born and brought up was, under the influence of Greek civilization. The Greek judiciary system required two witnesses to appear before a judge to bring evidence in a trial. God in His sovereignty, however, has provided us with four witnesses, all of whom are in agreement concerning the events of the life of Christ. II Corinthians 13:1 says, "...every fact is to be confirmed by the testimony of two or three witnesses."

Finally, the Bible is not a scientific book, but where it mentions science it is accurate. It is not a history book, but where it mentions anything historic it is again accurate. It is not a geography book, but where it mentions geography it has proven to be true and accurate. The Bible, as it is in our hands today, is the true Word of God and is able to stand up to any type of test, research, or criticism.

2. THE CONSISTENCY OF GOD'S REVELATION

In the Muslim mind, God has established three religions over the course of history: Judaism, Christianity, and Islam. Muslims believe that He first sent Moses to establish Judaism, but because the Jews were a stiff-necked, disobedient people He scattered them all over the world and sent Jesus, the son of Mary, to establish Christianity. By the fifth century, however, Christianity had become so corrupt that God sent Mohammad to establish Islam, His last and final revelation. Muslims believe that Islam includes both Judaism and Christianity, and they say that even Abraham was a Muslim. In their minds, Islam is everything and everything is Islam. What we need to explain to the Muslims - and it is not an easy task - is that God was consistent in His revelation and will continue to be so until the end.

God's primary purpose was not to establish a religion; religions are made by human beings. Rather, he wished to establish a personal relationship between Himself and man. This is the message of the entire Gospel. The first two chapters in the Bible speak about creation, including that of man and woman. In the third, we read about the fall of man into sin. From the fourth chapter of Genesis through to the end of the Book of Revelation, the primary message of God's Word is that of Salvation.

There is a very important passage in Genesis chapter 3, verses 14 and 15, in which God confronts Adam and Eve regarding their sin:

> And the Lord God said to the serpent,
> Because you have done this, cursed are you more
> than all cattle, and more than every beast of the field;
> on your belly you shall go, and dust shall you eat all

the days of your life;

And I will put enmity between you and the woman, And between your seed and her seed; He shall bruise you on the head, And you shall bruise him on the heel.

Take time to explain this passage *. Muslims already believe in the story of Adam and Eve, the creation and the fall. They also believe that Satan appeared in the shape of a serpent and tried to seduce the woman to eat from the fruit, that she succumbed to temptation and ate, and then she gave some of the fruit to her husband to eat. The key point here, however, is God's promise: *"...the seed of the woman shall bruise the head of Satan..."* If you ask a Muslim, "Who from the time of Adam and Eve until today was indeed born only from a woman *and* not from the union of a man and a woman?" they will say, "Jesus." They know this and believe it. Explain who the seed of the woman is, and also God's promise – that from the seed of the woman He would destroy Satan and redeem man. Explain that this promise, given the moment man fell into sin, was fulfilled by Jesus Christ.

You can also show how the prophets pointed their prophecies toward the coming of Christ. His coming was, from the beginning, part of God's plan:

Isaiah 7:14: "Behold, the virgin shall be found with child and bear a son, and she will call his name Emmanuel."

Isaiah 9:6: "For a child will be born to us, a son will

be given to us, and the government will rest on his shoulders, and his name will be called Wonderful Counselor, Mighty God, Eternal Father, Prince of Peace."

Matthew 1:23: "Behold, the virgin shall be with child, and shall bear a son, and they shall call his name Emmanuel, which translated means, 'God with us.'"

*Appendix A lists 45 Old Testament Messianic prophecies and their fulfillment in Christ.

3. WHY CHRISTIANS BELIEVE JESUS IS THE SON OF GOD

Is Jesus really the Son of God? The moment you begin speaking to a Muslim, typically the first and most offensive objection they have is that we say that Jesus is the Son of God. This is because when we say "Son of God" they think we are talking about a physical son (God having sexual relations with Mary), and this is blasphemy. We, too, believe this is blasphemy. You must clarify to the Muslim that when we say "Son of God" we do not believe that God ever had a physical relationship with a woman to have His son.

In explaining the Sonship of Christ to the Muslim, we need to tell them that Jesus is the Son of God from a spiritual point of view, not a physical one. Jesus is not the physical offspring of God. Refer to Luke chapter 1 and read together verses 26 through 35, about how the angel brought the news to Mary that she would conceive and give birth to a son. Pinpoint these important words to him: "The Holy Spirit will come upon you... So the holy one to be born will be called the Son of God." He is not the physical son of God, but we call him the Son of God because he came from the Spirit of God. Therefore, he is not the physical son, but "He shall be called the Son of God." Underline these words for him.

The second concept you need to understand and explain to the Muslim is that, especially in the Arabic version of the Bible, there is a big difference between the word "son" of God, and "child" of God. In Arabic, they are the words *ibn* and *walad*. Ibn means "son" and walad means "child." *Ibn* refers to the child you adopt; walad means it was born to you. This is why we never call Jesus in Arabic *WaladAllah*. We call Him *IbnAllah,* meaning He came from God. If the person you are sharing with is an Arab, ask him, "What is the difference between *ibn* and *walad?*" Let him think - see what he comes up with, and then explain the difference.

There is one other logical illustration you might give to the Muslim. In Arabic, the phrase "son of..." is used to signify where one is from. For instance, if I am from Lebanon, then I am called a "Son of Lebanon." A man from Morocco would be called a "Son of Morocco." And because the Nile is the most famous part of Egypt, an Egyptian will often be called "Son of the Nile." One could also be called "Son of Education," meaning that he is a very well educated person. The phrase may also be used to express one's main interest. In the same way, Christ is called "Son of God" because He came from the Spirit of God.

4. DID JESUS REALLY DIE ON THE CROSS?

A. Does the Qur'an refute Christ's crucifixion?

Muslims do not believe that Jesus died on the cross. There is a verse in the Qur'an which says, "They killed Him not, they crucified Him not, but it was likened unto them. They killed Him not knowingly, but God raised Him and God is the most merciful of merciful." Ninety percent of the time, the Muslim will tell me immediately, "But they killed Him not, they crucified Him not!" In the Muslim's mind, this verse is saying that God was so merciful that He could never allow a wonderful prophet such as Jesus to be crucified by His enemies.

In explaining the second part of the Qur'anic verse, which says, "They killed Him not knowingly," you can remind the person you're sharing with of the attitude the Jews held toward Christ. When Jesus was taken to the Roman governor, they did not believe He was the Messiah. They wanted to get rid of Him. So by saying, "They killed Him not knowingly," the Qur'anic verse is simply saying they killed Him without knowing He was the Messiah.

In fact, there are other verses in the Qur'an which state that Jesus was killed. One verse in particular attributes to Jesus the statement, "Peace unto Me the day I was born, the day I died and was taken to heaven."

B. The Biblical prophecy and necessity of Christ's crucifixion

The issue of Christ's death on the cross also brings

49

us back to the verses in Genesis 3:15. In this passage, God promised that the seed of the woman would bruise Satan, even though Satan would bruise His heel. The bruising of His heel is nothing less than His crucifixion and being nailed to the cross. But, though He was nailed to the cross, that same death would bruise Satan's head. Through this death and resurrection, Christ won the victory over Satan and redeemed mankind.

Also, in Genesis 4, we see how God accepted Abel's sacrifice, the lamb, but rejected Cain's sacrifice, which was the fruit of his labor. Explain to the person with whom you are sharing that the lamb is a substitute for man and represents the coming of Christ. The fruit of Cain's labor was representative simply of good works, and was not sufficient to meet God's requirement.

In Genesis 22, Abraham takes his son as a sacrifice in obedience to God's command: "And He said, 'Take now your son, your only son, whom you love, Isaac, and go to the land of Moriah; and offer him there as a burnt offering on one of the mountains of which I will tell you" (Genesis 22:2). What does this mean? Why would God have asked such a thing? Discuss the passage together, focusing especially on the picture of God providing a ram miraculously as a substitute for Abraham's son. Abraham had lifted his knife and was ready to kill his son, but what happened instead? He heard a voice saying, "Abraham! ... Do not stretch out your hand against the lad, and do nothing to him; for now

I know that you fear God, since you have not withheld your son, your only son, from Me" (Genesis 22:12). What would have happened had Abraham not listened? His son would have been killed. But Abraham believed and took instead the ram, which he sacrificed in the place of his son. You can explain that the ram represents Jesus Christ, and we can look back 2000 years ago and see Him on the cross for you and me. Turn to John 1:29, where John the Baptist proclaims, "Behold! The Lamb of God who takes away the sins of the world!" Jesus is the Lamb of God.

• There may be some argument here as to which son Abraham offered to the Lord. Muslims believe it was Ishmael, and this is important because Arabs are known to be the descendants of Ishmael. Because of this, the idea of God's redemption of Ishmael, while wrong in terms of scripture, is very important, because it signifies God's love for and redemption of the Arab race. Try to avoid a long, drawn-out discussion of this, and focus instead on the concept of Abraham taking his son and offering him to God. Whether Isaac or Ishmael, which son is not the issue.

In addressing the issue of Christ's death further, I strongly suggest you read through Isaiah 53, which very clearly speaks about the coming of Christ and the redemption of mankind – Jesus Himself bearing our sins on the cross, Himself being the sacrifice. The entire chapter talks about Jesus, but you should focus especially on verses 4 through 12.

Take time to underline all the prophecies regarding

Jesus. If possible, let the person you're sharing with read the passage first by himself, out loud. After he has read, ask him, "Who do you think the prophet Isaiah is talking about here?" He will most likely say that he is talking about the son of Mary, *Issa, Ibnou Mariam,* that is, Jesus, son of Mary. Christian Arabs call Him *Yassoua,* which is taken from *Yashoua,* the Hebrew name for Jesus, while Muslims call Him *Issa,* taken from *Yssus,* the Greek name for Jesus. Take this opportunity to show him that what was prophesied in Isaiah was fulfilled in the person of Christ nearly 600 years later.

Another important thing to point out here is that "the Lord was pleased" (verse 10) to offer Christ as a sacrifice for man's sin. God is just; He said in Romans 6:23, "For the wages of sin is death," which is eternal separation from God. However, God is also merciful. He would not allow the whole world to go to hell. From the moment man fell, the death and resurrection of Christ was planned as the solution for sin.

Now there are those who would question the necessity of Christ's death on the cross, citing good works as a means of atonement for one's sin. But suppose I stole your watch and you caught me, brought me to the police, and turned me in. Suppose further that because of this, the police sentenced me to five days in jail. Could I get out of it by saying, "Wait a minute. I bought him lunch yesterday, paid for his subway and everything!" Would this be sufficient to cancel out my crime? Would the police accept it? Of course not! It's not logical. Good works alone are not sufficient payment for one's crimes.

Here's an illustration of a just judge: A judge is sitting in the courtroom, wearing his judicial robe, and a young girl stands before him. She has been charged with driving without a license and speeding down the highway, for which the penalty is $500.00. He points his finger at her and asks, "Are you guilty or not?" To which she answers, "Yes, Your Honor; but I can't afford to pay the penalty." And with that dismisses the court. He then steps down from the bench, takes off his robe and gives the girl $500.00. Why? Because he is her father, and while he could not dishonor his name by letting her go free, he is also merciful and loving and could not bear to see her put in jail because of her inability to pay. The only solution, therefore, is for him to pay the penalty himself.

C. If Jesus died on the cross, and if Jesus is God, does that mean that God died on the cross also?

In the Gospel of John, chapter 4, we are told that God is Spirit. In the original Hebrew language, Spirit is *roh*. From this word, the word *rihe* is taken, which is also the air in the atmosphere. Air is everywhere. Though you cannot see it, you know it is present: You can feel it, you breathe it, even though it has no color or shape. The same thing is true with the Spirit of God – He is present everywhere.

If you take an empty bottle, you know that it is empty of any liquid, yet it is filled with air. The air that's inside the bottle, furthermore, has taken the shape of the bottle, even though air has no shape. The characteristics of the air inside the bottle are identical to the characteristics of the air outside the bottle. The fact that there is air inside the bottle does not mean there is none outside the bottle, because air exists everywhere in the atmosphere. Now, if you were to take the bottle today, and smash it against the wall, it would break into hundreds of little pieces. It would be shattered. Can we say that the air inside the bottle would also be shattered? No. Only the vessel that contained the air has been shattered.

The same thing took place when God, who is Spirit, dwelt among us in the body of Jesus Christ. God took the likeness of man. That does not mean that He no longer existed. Rather, like the air when it filled the bottle, God still exists everywhere. Furthermore, Jesus' crucifixion on the cross does not mean that God was killed, but rather that the body, which contained the Spirit of God, was killed. God has always existed, even during the three days in which Jesus was dead in the tomb. This is exactly what the Apostle Paul has written in his epistle to the Philippians, chapter 2, verses 5-11:

"Have this attitude in yourselves, which was also in Christ Jesus, who, although He existed in the form of God, did not regard equality with God a thing to be grasped, but emptied Himself, taking the form of a bond-servant, and being made in the likeness of men.

And being found in appearance as a man, He humbled Himself by becoming obedient to the point of death, even death on a cross. Therefore, also God highly exalted Him, and bestowed on Him the name which is above every name, that at the name of Jesus every knee should bow, of those who are in heaven, and on earth, and under the earth, and that every tongue should confess that Jesus Christ is Lord."

5. THE TRINITY

The final major issue which must be addressed with the Muslim is that of the Trinity. Muslims often say, "You Christians believe in three different gods - God the Father, Jesus, and the Holy Spirit. That is blasphemy! One cannot believe in three different gods." The task of helping a Muslim understand the Trinity is not an easy one - there are even many Christians who have a hard time explaining it. Take a molecule of H2O for example: It manifests itself in three different forms, liquid water, solid ice, and vaporous steam; but it is the same substance. Others use the sun illustration, the glowing ball of gases itself, the source, as representing God the Father; the radiating light represents Christ, the light of the world; and the heat that we feel represents the work of the Holy Spirit.

Regardless of which illustration you use, it's important to use the Word of God itself. Begin by establishing your belief in only one God. I Corinthians 8:4 says, "There is no God but one," Then follow up by sharing as many verses as possible which illustrate the Trinity.

Appendix B will help you better communicate the

doctrine of the Trinity. Each of the passages cited refers to attributes which are possessed only by God, such as His holiness and His unchanging and eternal nature. They also refer to functions, such as baptism and salvation, for which only He is responsible. As you share these verses, note that each person of the Trinity is said to possess each of these attributes and is involved in each of these functions. It therefore follows that either all three persons are God, or all three are One.

Please remember that we are not trying to win an argument, nor are we out to prove the other person wrong. Rather, it is the Gospel we wish to share and explain to the Muslim. Avoid all forms of arguments and debates and seek to explain the Gospel and answer any questions a Muslim may have, especially pertaining to the five basic issues discussed here. As Peter said in his epistle:

> *"...but sanctify Christ as Lord in your hearts, always being ready to make a defense to everyone who asks you to give an account for the hope that is in you, yet with gentleness and reverence."*
>
> —1 Peter 3:15

As we give an answer, let us trust that the Word of God, which is living and active, will minister to our friends through the power of the Holy Spirit and lead them to know the Way, the Truth, and the Life through Jesus Christ our Lord.

At this point, you may have some argumentative

Muslims who will tell you that the Bible actually talks about the coming of Mohammad, not just Christ. They will ask you why you do not also believe in Mohammad. You need to ask them which verses talk about the coming of Mohammad. Most likely you will end up returning to the issue of the authenticity of the Bible, and whether or not it has been changed. Some Muslims, however, if they have really studied and learned a lot, will point to the prophecy Jesus gave: "I will send you the Comforter." In Greek, the word "Comforter" is "Paracletos." If this word is changed just a bit to "Paracletas" – in Arabic it would mean "Mahmood," which has the meaning "being thanked" or "thankful." This has the same root as Mohammad. They will say that the Bible was changed from saying, "I will send you Mohammad," to "I will send you the Comforter." In John, chapters 14 and 16 however, we see that the word "Paracletos" is never used by itself. Whenever Christ speaks of the Comforter in these chapters, He always says who He is – the Spirit of truth. Take time to read these verses with your friend. If the Muslim is really enjoying the discussion, read right through into Acts 2, when the Spirit of truth actually comes to the disciples.

It is not necessary for you to become knowledge-able of the whole content of the Qur'an, although it would be profitable if you are able to read it as well as any other books you can find on witnessing to Muslims. There are, however, two schools of thought concerning the use of the Qur'an in Muslim evangelism. One says that verses from the Qur'an should always be used, and the other says that they should never be used. The first group believes that using the Qur'an will prove the accuracy of the Bible; while the latter believes this will bring the Qur'an up to the same level as the Bible. The typical Muslim might say, "If the Qur'an proves what you are saying, then I will continue believing in it, since it includes the same things – so why do I need the Bible?" Regardless of which school of thought you adhere to, it is important for a Muslim to know you understand Islam. In this particular case, it is crucial that you understand the verse and where it comes from.

SOME PRACTICAL TIPS

• Start by being a friend and loving him or her. If a Muslim trusts Christ, he will need a strong support network of Christians, because he may well be cut off entirely from his family and friends.

• DO NOT COMPARE BOOKS. Even if you are an expert on the Hebrew and Christian Bibles, the Qur'an, other sacred literature, and the transmission thereof, do *NOT* compare books. Muslim reasoning regarding the Qur'an is highly circular. Prophets can only be called prophets in Islam if they performed miracles. Since Muhammad did not perform any miracles, the Qur'an is said to be his miracle, and this is said to be self-evident. Don't bother debating. You will both waste your time and drive away your Muslim friends.

• Sharing Christ step-by-step (a brief outline): Ask your friend what he or she already knows about Christianity. Many Muslims have completely distorted views of what Christians believe, while others may understand some of the basics quite well. Be sure to ask what questions your friend has.

KEY CONCEPTS FOR SALVATION:

• Sacrifice is necessary for forgiveness, because all have sinned. It is often not necessary to read Romans 3:23 or 6:23 here, as Muslims will generally agree without hesitation that all are sinners – except prophets, but don't get into that – and that the penalty for sin is death.

• Jesus is the only sufficient sacrifice since he was a sinless man. Avoid discussion of the Trinity when first sharing. It is not comprehensible from a Muslim standpoint, and will only make matters harder. *Do* stress that you agree that there is only one God; Islam teaches that Christianity is a form of polytheism. The driving idea here is that sinful people cannot redeem themselves.

• God's love can only be known through Jesus' sacrifice. This is a personal relationship. Stress that God *does* love them and died for them specifically. See 1 John 3:16.

• Start with the sacrifice of Abraham's son and God's provision of a substitute *(Eid al-Adha)*. Muslims believe this was Ishmael, not Isaac – don't haggle over names. Stress the concept: one sacrifice to save one person.

• Talk about Passover. Muslims know the Exodus story, though in a corrupted form, so they are familiar with this: one sacrifice to save one family. The story is in Exodus 12.

• Yom Kippur, the Day of Atonement. This is the annual day that the Jewish High Priest would enter the Holy of Holies after performing a sacrifice to take away the sins of the entire nation. Muslims are also familiar with this. One sacrifice for one nation.

• Explain that Jesus is the last and greatest sacrifice for the whole world. (Hebrews 10:12)

• Read Isaiah 53. Ask, "Who does this refer to?" Oddly, though Islam vehemently denies that Christ suffered or died, Muslims will almost always immediately recognize that this refers to Jesus. Then tell them that it was written 700 years before Christ.

• Stress love and grace through Christ, not Christianity as a religion or any specific doctrines beyond sin and repentance; the rest will come in time.

• If your friend is receptive, watch the *JESUS* film with him or her. Be sure to be available to field questions, and don't forget to pray!

Pray . . .

• About how God would use you in fulfilling the Great Commission among Muslims.

• For laborers for the harvest. (Matthew 9:37-38, Luke 10:2-3)

• For believers and non-believers in the Muslim

world, where conversion to Christianity is often punished (legally or illegally) by death. Pray for greater freedom in spreading the Gospel into these countries and for mutual understanding between Christians and Muslims.

SUMMARY

In witnessing to a Muslim, remember to be filled with the Holy Spirit. Be covered and indwelt. Be strengthened.

Secondly, begin with PRAYER. Pray for guidance and protection for yourself. Pray for the Holy Spirit to intervene. Keep in mind that Islam is NOT just a religion, but a spiritual force that is not of the true and living God. Islam offers no freedom from sin, no hope for eternal security, no cleansing. So, what is the big draw? It MUST be this ungodly spiritual force that drives it. That means one must be absolutely bathed in prayer before, during, and after witnessing to a Muslim.

Thirdly, go to your Muslim friend in love. Find authentic ways to demonstrate your Christian compassion. Do not go with an attitude of superiority or condemnation. Do not put down Muhammad. Do not go with the intent of winning a debate-you will not win. You must be knowledgeable about scriptures, and you must be accurate in your understanding about what Muslims believe. Use scriptures and let the Holy Spirit's power work.

Finally, be patient. Expect to hear illogical explanations,

inaccurate retelling of Bible stories, and misquoting of key verses. Also expect to hear superstitions given the full stature of Holy Scripture. Many Muslims freely admit that they are superstitious; some are not. In any case, the cultures of the Muslim world have many superstitious practices which are hard to overcome. So, please be prepared to be patient, kind, and loving.

Memorize this quote from the Qur'an 10:94, "If thou wert in doubt as to what we have revealed unto thee, then ask those who have been reading The Book (the Bible) before thee." This is referring to Christians and Jews. If a Muslim doesn't understand the Bible, Muhammad said to go to those who do – the Christians and Jews. It's right in their Qur'an.

Be patient, and be prepared. Seek the Holy Spirit's favor, guidance, wisdom, and protection.

So…Be filled. Pray. Love. Be patient. *Then* share.

Reaching Out With Love

AN INTRODUCTORY BIBLE STUDY

INTRODUCTION

• Islam (the Arabic word for "surrender") is the fastest growing religion in America and the entire world, with approximately 1 billion adherents. There are more American Muslims than Methodists.

• A practitioner of Islam is a Muslim if male, Muslimah if female.

• Islam is often confused with being Arabic. The Arabs are best defined as the people of the world whose primary language is Arabic. Not all Arabs are Muslims; not all Muslims are Arabic.

• Islam was founded by Muhammad, who lived in what is now Saudi Arabia, in about A.D. 622, the traditional date for the *hijrah,* or "flight" of Muhammad from Mecca to

Medina, and the date used to divide the Muslim calendar.

MAJOR BELIEFS:

• Islam is seen as the perfect, final religion for all mankind, not a new religion, but the same one taught by all true prophets, including Moses *(Musa)*, Jesus *(Isa)*, Abraham *(Ibrahim)*, Lot, Aaron, Solomon, Job, and others. Of course, if the Bible and Qur'an contradict – and they do – then Islam and Christianity cannot both be true religions.

• STRICTLY Monotheistic: Christianity is seen as polytheistic by Muslims because of the Trinity. All Muslims believe in one transcendent, omniscient, omnipotent God, called Allah. *[Note: Allah is the only word in Arabic for God. Though the Muslim and Christian concepts of God are very different, Arabic Christians and Muslims both call God Allah. Christians, however, sometimes refer to God as Ar-Rabb (the Lord) or Al-Masih (Christ), for clarity.]* In Islam, the one unpardonable sin is *shirk,* association of others with God. (Compare the Bible: though even Jacob and Solomon committed idolatry, they were forgiven. Still, in Acts 15:20, idolatry was one of only four sins the apostles felt they needed to mention in a letter to the Gentile converts, showing that God's abhorrence of idolatry is by no means limited to Old Testament times. See Matthew 12:31-37.)

• Muhammad is seen as the last and greatest, the "seal" of the prophets; Jesus, the Messiah *(al-masih)*, is second. Muhammad is *NOT* considered divine, though he is an intercessor for Muslims on the Day of Judgment. He is not guaranteed salvation by Allah; however, Muslims are asked to pray to him fifty times on Fridays. Muhammad was given a book (as are all prophets, including Jesus, who was supposedly *given* the Gospel in its original, "pure" form). Muhammad's book is called *Al-Qur'an,* "the recitation" (sometimes spelled Qur'an). Muslims often claim that Moses's promise of "a prophet like me from your midst" (Deuteronomy 18:15, NKJV) predicts the coming of Muhammad. Many also claim that the "paraclete" ("Helper," which refers to the Holy Spirit) of John 14:16 originally read "Muhammad" and was changed by early Christians. This chain of prophecy is important to Muhammad's claim to authority, but is entirely fabricated.

• Day of Judgment: At the end of the world, all people will be judged by their earthly actions, but no one, including Jesus or Muhammad, is guaranteed salvation. That is solely according to the will of Allah. Contrast Romans 10:9, "If you confess with your mouth the Lord Jesus and believe in your heart that God has raised Him from the dead, you will be saved" (NKJV); and 1 John 5:13, "I have written to you who believe in the name of the Son of God that you may know that you have eternal life, and that you may continue to believe in the name of the Son of God" (NKJV). Biblical salvation – by faith in Christ – and Qur'anic salvation – by faith in the Qur'an, strict legalism, and the whim of Allah – are not compatible.

MAJOR PRACTICES:

- **The Five Pillars**
- **Shahada** – "to bear witness", especially by reciting the confession of faith: "There is no God but God, and Muhammad is his prophet." This is the first thing a newborn hears and the last phrase whispered to the dying. Saying it sincerely is sufficient to make one a Muslim. This goes well beyond a statement such as the Apostle's Creed, in that it is both mandatory and completely standardized throughout the Muslim world.

- **Salat** – prayer; mandatory minimum of five times a day. Muslim prayer is very scripted: one must wash oneself in a ritual manner, then perform a series of bows and prostrations while reciting and listening to passages from the Qur'an and the liturgy, usually at a mosque, with other Muslims. The prayers are fixed passages of the Qur'an; compare Matthew 6:5-15.

- **Sawm** – religious fast during the Islamic month of Ramadan; mandatory. Compare Matthew 6:16-18.

- **Zakat** – alms; mandatory (often by law) minimum of two and a half percent of one's income. Compare Matthew 6:1-4.

- **Hajj** – pilgrimage to Mecca; mandatory for all able believers once in their lifetime and performed as a group during Ramadan. [Approximately 2 million people a year perform the Hajj, which is coordinated by the Saudi Arabian government, with assistance from other

Muslim nations.] Compare Acts 7:44–50.

• **Jihad** – "struggle". Sometimes called the "sixth pillar." There are two kinds of *jihad*.

• **Lesser** *jihad* ("the jihad of the sword") refers to military force. It is commanded and permissible only when Muslims are oppressed and prohibited from worshipping freely. Compare Matthew 5:38–48.

• **Greater** *jihad* ("the *jihad* of the heart") refers to a personal struggle for righteousness.

MAJOR WRITINGS:

• The *Qur'an,* or "recitation"

• The only sacred or inspired book of Islam. (The Bible is *Al-Kitab Al-Qudus,* "The Holy Book.")

• Contains 114 chapters *(surat),* each ranging from half a dozen verses *(ayat)* to about three hundred.

• Believed to have been dictated to Muhammad by the archangel Gabriel over twenty-three years. The Qur'an on earth today, though compiled from very small fragments and many early versions, is held to be a letter-perfect copy of an original in heaven. After the first revelation, *Muhammad originally was sure he had been possessed by a demon.* His first wife, Khadija, convinced him otherwise. Still, several years had passed before Muhammad began to teach. [This is problematic for the Muslim assertion that all prophets prophesied willingly; the book of Jonah doesn't help this claim either].

• Proclaims the unity (*ahad,* "oneness" of God, absolute one, and *wahid,* "one" or "the same" [God for all people]) of Allah and denies Him any partners (such as sons).

• Written in extremely archaic Cufic Arabic, believed to be the language of God [Q:"Why?" A:"Because the Qur'an says so." Q: "Why should we believe the Qur'an?" A:"It is the best book in Arabic, and Arabic is the language of God." Q:"Says who?" A:"The Qur'an." Etc.]

• The *hadith,* or "stories" (non-written forms are called *sunna,* "traditions of the prophet")

• Thousands exist. Muslims universally reject many of them, yet no authoritative test exists for determining which are to be rejected (only about twenty percent are universally accepted). They all trace themselves through early Muslim leaders to Muhammad himself, and some of the "best" trails include false traditions. The *hadith* has been called "the key to the lock of the Qur'an" and many *hadith* are considered to be inspired by God to help Muslims understand the Qur'an.

KEY QUESTION:

Why are the sayings of Muhammad in the hadith, if they are inspired by God, instead of the Qur'an or another holy book? How do you know the Qur'an is inspired, if many hadith which claim to be inspired are not?

SOME MUSLIM BELIEFS ABOUT:

JESUS:

• Not the Son of God. Muslims think this means God had relations with Mary, which is blasphemous to them as well as to Christians; see instead Luke 1:26-38, where it is clear that God's *power* is the source of Mary's child, not a physical union.

• Merely a prophet, one of 144,000, though he is given the title of *al-Masih,* "the anointed one," or Messiah, but not at all in a Christian sense. Compare Matthew 11:9, Matthew 16:3-17, where Christ himself claims to be more than a prophet.

• Born of a virgin. See Luke 1, though the Muslim stories, even in the Qur'an, vary in many details.

• Sinless, but in the sense that all prophets in Islam are sinless. Not perfect. (One Muslim man explained that Jesus was not perfect because he could still stub his toes or accidentally look at certain portions of the female anatomy or an idol, but never purposely sinned.)

• Does not atone for anyone's sins. See Isaiah 53: 4-6,10; Ephesians 1:3-7.

• Did not suffer or die. Most Muslims believe that Allah made somebody else, maybe Judas Iscariot, *look* like Jesus and die in his place. See 1 Corinthians 15:3-8.

• Believed to be really named *Isa,* a corrupted form of Esau, which Muslims believe, is a corrupted form of Ishmael. (The Qur'an confuses Ishmael and Isaac with almost perfect consistency. Ishmael, Abraham's other son, is

71

very likely the father of all the Arab nations).

• Will come again near the end of time, slay all the pigs of the world, proclaim Islam, have children, and die (This is not an orthodox belief, though it is widely held).

GOD OR ALLAH

• Perfect, just, sinless, forgiving, etc.

• Infinite

• Creator

• Merciful (though mercy to a Muslim means a kind of whimsical mercy which Allah may withdraw at any point. There is absolutely no assurance of salvation).

• Has 99 "most beautiful" names, which are often paradoxical (i.e., "the Hidden" *al-Batin* and "the Manifest" *az-Zahir*).

• Has no sons, daughters, wives, partners, etc. (Again, the Qur'an's insistence on this point derives in part from the misunderstanding of the term "Son of God.")

THE BIBLE

• Composed of *tawrat* (Torah), *zabur* (Psalms of David), and *injil* (Gospels, or sometimes entire New Testament), though these terms sometimes refer to books which have never existed [For example, the *injil* is believed to be a book, essentially like the Qur'an, *given* to Jesus, as opposed to the Gospels, which are and have always been *about* Jesus].

• God's inspired Word, but changed or corrupted *(tahrif)* by sinful men, especially Jews and Christians, including Paul. [Compare 2 Timothy 3:16-17, Matthew 5:18, Revelation 22:18.] Supposedly, however, the "original" Bible and the Qur'an are equal in terms of authority (see Qur'an 2:132,136, and 5:114).

KEY QUESTIONS:

Why does Muhammad tell Christians, his own followers, and even himself to consult the tawrat and injil of his day if they are corrupted (Qur'an 5:50, 10:94)? How is it that the Bible was corrupted by men, if it was God's word (the same message as the Qur'an), but the Qur'an was not?

• Is sometimes selectively quoted. Often, Muslims reject part of a verse but not the rest. For example (Islam-compatible portions underlined): "In the beginning was the Word, and the Word was with God, and the Word was God. He [It] was with Him in the beginning. Through Him [it] all things were made…In Him [it] was life…" (John 1:1-4). There is no agreement on which parts are legitimate. Why are certain portions rejected? Those are the portions which contradict the Qur'an!

• Is believed to testify to the coming of Muhammad as the greatest prophet or apostle (esp. Deuteronomy 18:15-18), rather than Jesus.

SIN AND SALVATION

- Sin includes failing the Five Pillars.

- Salvation is dependent upon obedience. Missed prayers, for example, can be made up by doing extra prayers in the future. Compare Ephesians 2:8-9.

- Salvation is by the choosing, or whim, of Allah.

- No one can actually make up for sin entirely; only improve his/her balance. (Compare Hebrews 9:16-22, 10:4) It is impossible to atone for even the tiniest sin through sacrifice.

- Atonement for sins is acknowledged in *Eid al-Adha,* the holiday commemorating Abraham's willingness to sacrifice his son (Ishmael, in the Qur'an).

The more information you have, the better prepared you will be for whatever questions may arise as you seek to reach out to those of the Islamic faith.

WHY I BECAME A CHRISTIAN

Without active missionary efforts, most of the world's Muslims will never hear the gospel. In some places, less than 1 in 100 million Muslims will ever hear the truth.

The ultimate goal in reaching out to Muslims is to lead them to a saving knowledge of Jesus Christ. Up to this point, we have told you the basics of Islam and what differences there are in reaching Muslims compared to reaching non-Muslims. But basically, the only thing that matters is that those who follow Islam are sinners in need of grace—just like you and me. God's arms are open to every sinner who comes to Him, proclaims Jesus as Lord, and accepts the forgiveness God is offering. Below are three testimonies of former Muslims who learned about Jesus and accepted His grace. I pray that they will inspire you to reach out to Muslims in your life.

WHY I BECAME A CHRISTIAN

I was born in Saudi Arabia as a member of a Muslim family. We were a very happy family, and I loved my relationship with them. I also felt very happy because I did all the things that God asked me to. I had learned one sixth of the holy Qur'an by heart and a lot from the Hadith. When I was a teenager, I was an Imam for the mosque.

I was always very serious to do all that God ordered me to do—fasting during Ramadan, praying five times a day or more, Hajj, and so on. I, at that time, very much desired to meet God at the last day, even when I had no guarantee. But I had always hoped for this. My hope grew when I started to think about fighting in the name of God (Jihad) in Afghanistan. I was sixteen years old. My parents would not let me go because I was too young. So I decided to wait until I was old enough.

I always had love and respect for the Muslim people. There was no love or respect in my heart for the Christians, and the Jews were my first enemy, of course.

FAR AWAY FROM GOD

After some time, the devil found his way into our home and our life, and my life became very hard. Slowly I drifted far away from God until the time that I believed in no God at all.

My life became busy. I had a very good job and earned a lot of money. Still, I was not happy because I was afraid for the day that I would die. Sometimes a question came to my mind — will I be with God in heaven or not? And it was very frightening to think about this, even for seconds, that I would not be there. What about my future?

A Little Prayer

One day I had a big problem in my life. I was in my room looking through the window up to the sky. Then I remembered God, and I wanted to pray to him to ask him for help, but which God should I pray to. Allah? I was sure that he was very angry with me because I had not prayed for a very long time. Or Jesus? I knew He had done a lot of miracles in the lives of other people. Then I said, "Jesus help me!" I don't know why I spoke like this. I sat down on my bed and spoke to myself, "What is this stupid thing you just did?" Anyway, I did not expect anything to happen or the problem to go away. However, one and a half days later, my problem was solved! I decided to find out who this Jesus is. Is he God as the Christian people say, or is he a prophet, as I know from Islam? At this time, I left my country and went to Europe.

The Dream

On the third day, my circumstances became very

difficult for me, and I decided to go back to the Middle East. During that night I had a dream. I was standing in a cross shape with a low wall around it. In my right hand, I had a big stack of white, unwritten papers. I was standing at the cross beam, and I was looking to a small group of people who were standing at the top. They all wore long, white clothing, but one of them was different. He was standing at the right side, and with his left hand he was leading the people through a door in the wall. Beyond the door was light, and I could not see what was in there. One moment I was standing in the dream, and the next moment I was seeing the cross from above. It was difficult for me to understand this.

When I woke up the next morning, I felt a very beautiful happiness in my heart that I never had before. And I felt a love in my heart and from inside my body a very special feeling. I felt also I just wanted to walk and to walk and to ask everyone I met, do you know Jesus?

It was more than a great feeling. It was happiness that I had never known before in my life.

After one year of reading the Bible in an honest way, I understand now what happened to me. I found my way to God, the real God, the Lord Jesus Christ. I hope now for all the people I love, my family, my friends, and everyone else to change also and begin to read the Bible in an honest way. I am sure that God will help them to find their way.

MY LIFE NOW

I feel love in my heart, and I am very happy to know Jesus. When I was a Muslim, I could never imagine that the Christians were right. After that, I found out how much God loves me, and I became a Christian. Yes, He loves me, He loves you, and He loves the whole world. Jesus Christ loved us, and He still does. And don't forget in the last day nobody else can save us, only Jesus Christ.

Dear brother/sister,

Come to know Jesus before it is too late. John 8:12: When Jesus spoke again to the people, he said, "I am the light of the world. Whoever follows me will never walk in darkness, but will have the light of life."

Feel free to write me at : Desertson@exmuslim.com

Testimonies of Former Muslims

BASSAM'S TESTIMONY

I live in the Middle East. I was born as a Muslim, and at the age of 18 I became a member of one of the Islamic groups, as I had a relative who was one of the leaders of this group. I thought I was doing everything I could for God as I knew him at this point.

After a short time I started to get some training in using guns and making explosives. I wasn't very comfortable with what I was doing - hurting people for God's sake. I thought that either I or the group had misunderstood the teachings of God. I started to study the Qur'an and the Hadith all over again, (with the help of one of the leaders of the group, without telling him my real reasons for studying) to see what I had missed. After a couple of years, I was astonished at what I found. I found that Islam is not the peaceful path to God as I used to believe; on the contrary, it's so violent. If I have to establish God's will by any means possible, even by killing people, I said it can't be the way to God.

I never considered myself leaving Islam for anything else, yet at this point I was sure that it wasn't leading me to God. I had a kind of breakdown for some time when I found that everything I had believed in wasn't right; I started doing drugs and not talking about God at all.

Then I met a Christian who didn't know much of the Christian theology but who was full of love to others, whatever and whoever they are. One of his friends (who was a member of the same group that I had been involved in) said about him that he must be killed because he was Christian and didn't pay *Jiziah* (tax levied on Christians and Jews in an Islamic state, according to the Qur'an), yet this didn't stop him loving this man or dealing with him professionally. Initially I didn't know he was Christian, and when I found out I was surprised; everything I had learned all my life about Christians from my reading of Islamic writings and Muhammad's opinion about them put them down very much. I asked this friend if I could have a copy of the Bible.

After starting to read the Bible I found a very big difference between what is actually written in the Bible and what I had heard people (Muslims and even nominal Christians) say about it.

I was really struck by one thing in the Bible, namely

the teaching that no one is righteous but Jesus; even those who were called God's people like David, Jacob and Abraham, the twelve apostles – everyone has done something wrong. The Bible is full of the sins and wrongdoing of all people, except Jesus. He himself said to his enemies "Which of you convicts me of sin?" (John 8:46a), and no one responded. Even Judas Iscariot, who delivered him up to the authorities to be killed, said "I have sinned in betraying innocent blood" (Matthew 27:4). In addition, Pontius Pilate, the Roman governor who eventually did sentence him to death, said "Why, what evil has he done? I have found in him no crime deserving death." And then a centurion who witnessed Jesus' death said, "Certainly this man was innocent!" He struck me as the highest example of a human being, one who really deserved to be followed. It took me some time till I finished the whole Bible. After about one year of hard struggle with myself, I decided that I wanted to follow God as He shows himself in Christ, not as anyone else says He is.

I prayed to Him and He was here; for the first time in my life I felt that God was here, and to say it was a very strange feeling for me would be an understatement. I was so happy, so sad. Happy to know He is here and sad for what I had missed. It felt very peaceful and I wanted this feeling to last for good. I still remember this very first time I prayed; I ran out of the room because for the first time in my life I felt the presence of God. I have been following Him since then. He changed all my life. I went off drugs; I became a whole new person to everyone that I know, but as I said before, I live in the Middle East where everyone thinks that he IS RIGHT and everyone else is wrong, so I had some trouble with my family and they kicked me out of the house. As Jesus says, "Brother will deliver up brother to death, and the father his child, and children will rise against parents and have them put to death" (Matthew 10:21), and that is what happened with me.

My father delivered me to the Security Forces and they arrested me and put me in prison for converting out of Islam. I had a very bad time there, as they tortured me to force me to return to Islam. They used electric shocks, beatings, and hanging me from my wrists all night. After a few weeks of this I was put in solitary confinement for almost a year. But I couldn't deny the One who gave me life. Now I am out of jail and I have left my home country as I am still wanted there for apostasy from Islam. I am still walking with Jesus, and I love Him because He loved me first and put Himself on the cross for me. I knew from the very beginning that I was going to have some trouble; didn't He say about Paul "for I will show him how much he must suffer for the sake of my name." (Acts 9:16)

Now I am free from everything. I have a lovely wife whom I met after getting out of prison, and who is supporting me in everything I do for God, but the most important thing for me is I have my eternal assurance that

I am going to be with Him forever, whatever might happen. And as a result I decided to spend my life telling people about his great love to us. As he ordered me, "Do not be afraid, but speak and do not be silent; for I am with you, and no man shall attack you to harm you; for I have many people in this city." (Acts 18:9, 10)

Please feel free to write me if you want to know more, my email address is bassam@thompsonic.com.

THE STRAIGHT PATH

I was born to Muslim parents, and I'm a descendant of 'Ali Ibn Abu Talib, the cousin of Mohammad, the prophet of Islam, and the fourth Caliph (i.e., "ruler").

At an early age, I was one of the Muslim believers who performed all of the religious duties, from praying to fasting and everything in between. I was planning to be an Imam of a mosque, like my grandfather. I started to study the Fiqh and the Qur'an (Islamic sacred scripture), but after some time, I felt bored reading similar books and essays. I recognized that there are a lot of differences in Islam. For instance, in Iraq (my country), there are a lot of Shia, and it was strange for a Sunni like me to know that there was someone different from his faith but claiming to be

Muslim, so I decided to study the various Islamic schools of thought.

After a lot of reading in this field, I become more familiar with Mu'tazilah than any other school of thought. Mu'tazilah is more reasonable than the rest of the schools, in the sense that it involves argumentation and philosophy.

I began to be open-minded for the first time in my life. Gradually, I decided to study other religions. I tried to preach the Qur'an, starting in Da'wa (i.e., evangelism) with some young Christians, using my good knowledge of the argumentative tools, and I created many faith problems for them. Because of this, their families appealed to the priest of their church and asked him to invite me to visit him.

Arguing with him was very difficult for me because he always answered all my doubting questions. After I had known him a year, he died, but he had changed a lot of my thoughts about Christianity. However, I still didn't believe in it.

After this, I started to see Islam with new eyes, seeing the contradictions in it, studying it in comparison to Christianity.

One night in a dream, I saw a vision of a man with a beard talking to me:

"Son," he asked me, "why do you attack my sheep?"

I replied, "Who are you, sir?"

He answered, "Jesus Christ."

So, I answered his question, "I'm not attacking your

sheep, sir, I'm trying to bring your lost sheep back to the straight path."

He said, "You are the one who is lost; I'm the straight path."

I woke up asking myself a number of questions: Did I really see Jesus? He said that I'm lost. What did He mean? Does that mean that the Christian is right and that I'm on the wrong path? But it was only a dream. Still, Mohammad said in one of his Hadith that if you see a prophet in a dream, you see him truly because Satan could not act like a prophet in a vision. Obey him, and follow what he says. That is what Mohammad said.

After some time being a little confused, I left the two religions and became a non-believer.

Around that time, my father (a high-ranking officer) died in a car accident, which we assumed was a natural accident. So, I kept carrying on with my life, and because I had inherited from my father a good fortune, I was able to do a lot of wicked things - wasting money on sex, alcohol, drugs, and whatever I could find for pleasure.

After a period of time, I heard again a voice (which I knew was Jesus' voice), saying, "Run away from your country NOW!"

This voice was firm with me, so I woke up, I bagged my things, and in a few hours, I was outside Iraq and heading for my mother's home in another Arabic country.

When I was in the airplane (that was 1990, and Iraq

was not under the siege), I began to doubt my actions and started to blame myself for the stupid thing I was doing. But then, I told myself, "Well, let's have an early vacation. I can at least thank Jesus for that." And I smiled at the evil thoughts about what I was going to do for pleasure on my trip.

When I landed in the Arabic country that I was traveling to, I went to my grandfather's house. There, I called my mother back in Iraq saying, "Mom, don't worry. I'm visiting here for a while, and then I'll return home."

She replied, "Don't ever think about coming back. There was a police unit seeking you!"

Knowing that I had never broken the law or even been involved in any political opposition, I answered in shock, "What? What you are talking about?"

She said, "They were seeking some military documents that they think that your father hid, and for this (they had told her), he was assassinated. Thank God that you left. They thought that you had the documents. They took your brothers (from another mother), too, to investigate them."

[Note: My mother was protected during all of this because she was an Arabic journalist working with her country's embassy, so nobody could hurt her or arrest her for investigation without permission from the ministry of foreign affairs.]

I was shocked. I felt dizzy. I could not imagine what would happen! But if I were there in Iraq, they would torture me to confess what I had not done, and maybe they would kill me. What an unexpected danger I had escaped from! I had never imagined that I would have to flee for my life. I had never had a thought that I could ever be in such danger.

Who could have known such a future for me?! God alone could have known it! So, was Jesus God?!! I really became confused, shocked, dizzy, and - in this condition - passed out. After a few hours, I woke up from my comatose state, and I started to pray to God, sincerely asking Him to show me the way, the truth.

After that, I dreamed again of Jesus, and He said to me, "I love you. Why don't you love me likewise? Come to me because I have a plan for you." I woke up crying. He was looking for me, and I was trying to escape from Him. He wanted me to be with Him, and I was not. He had saved me from the hands of the Iraqi torture machine, so I told Him, "I'm coming to you, Jesus, even if this costs me my life."

At that moment, He entered my life, and become my Lord and Savior. I really was washed in His pure blood, becoming another person. I experienced His joy and peace, and became one reborn in His grace.

The only real worry that I had, however, was about my means of living, for I had left my wealth behind me, and unfortunately for me, the Iraqi authorities had confiscated all my property.

But the Lord showed me that I couldn't rely upon

material wealth anyway, for a few months later, Iraq invaded Kuwait, and the Iraqi Dinar, which was officially three dollars and in the black market merely 30 cents, fell enormously in value. Most of the wealth that I had inherited from my father had been in Iraqi currency, and I had it in the bank while I was living in Iraq. If I had still been living in Iraq during the Gulf crisis, then instead of having $300,000, I would have had only $300!! Thanks be to Jesus for showing me that I can only depend upon him, not upon worldly things. From this, I derive comfort.

After a long period of time in my mother's country, where I was witnessing for Jesus, extremist Islamic groups there discovered my apostasy from Islam. They held a faith court about me, and commanded me to repent and renew my faith in Islam, or they would kill me for being a Murtadd ("apostate"). They gave me two days to make my decision.

I tried to go to the police for protection, but the police arrested me for inciting activities against Islam and disturbing community security. They put me in jail and started to investigate me, asking about other converts and about missionaries. I was lucky that I had not been baptized yet because they emphasized the following questions: "Have you ever been baptized?!" "Who baptized you?!" "Which church do you attend?!" "Who evangelized you?!"

My being a foreigner helped me, for they eventually released me and commanded me to leave the country, giving me only a very short period in which to do so. God provided me a visa to a safe country, and I left my mother's country within the time they had demanded.

I'm seeking asylum now in a safe country, so please pray for me to get asylum - and pray for my mother, too, for she is still a Muslim, and I don't know when I will ever see her again. Unfortunately, I'm her only son, and I was her only financial source till I left.

May God bless you, and guide you to His truth.

Abdelrahman

Update, three years later: After many court trials, and having suffered rejections in several countries in my request for asylum as a religious refugee, I finally live now in a safe place the Lord provided for me.

If you would like to contact me, feel free to send me an e-mail at khaled@exmuslim.com

CONCLUSION

"Our struggle is not against flesh and blood, but against the rulers, against the authorities, against the powers of this dark world and against the spiritual forces of evil in heavenly realms"
(Ephesians 6:12).

We are to love the Muslims around us and pray for God's work in their lives. Be strong in the Lord and in His mighty power. Go forth in the power of His love and strength, knowing that witnessing is not "bringing people to the Lord" so much as it is simply telling those for whom He lived and died what He has done for you and about the Good News of Jesus Christ. Dr. Bill Bright, founder of Campus Crusade for Christ, said it well: "witness in the power of the Holy Spirit—*leaving the results to God.*"

APPENDIX A

Old Testament Messianic Prophecies

45 Major Prophecies

Prophecies beyond the control of Jesus in Bold

Fulfillment in Italics

I. HIS HUMAN ORIGINS

1. **Born of the seed of woman;** Gen. 3:15; *Matt. 1:20 & Gal. 4:4*
2. **Seed of Abraham;** Gen. 22:13; *Matt. 1:1 & Gal. 3:16*
3. **Son of Isaac;** Gen. 21:12; *Luke 3:23,24 & Matt. 1:2*
4. **Son of Jacob;** Numbers 24:17; *Luke 3:23,34, 1:33 & Matt. 1:2*
5. **From the tribe of Judah;** Gen. 49:10 & Micah 5:2; *Luke 3:23, 33 & Matt. 1: 2 & Heb. 7: 14*
6. **From the family line of Jesse;** Isaiah 11:1,10; *Luke 3:23,32 & Matt. 1:6*
7. **From the house of David; Jeremiah** 23:5 & 1 Chronicles

17:11-14; *Matt.1:1 & Mark 10:47-48 & Luke 3:23,31 & Acts 13:22-23 & Rev. 22:16*

II. HIS BIRTH

1. **Born of a virgin;** Isaiah 7:14; *Matt. 1:18,24,25 & Luke 1:26-35*
2. **Born in Bethlehem;** Micah 5:2; *Matt. 2:1,4-8 & John 7:42 & Luke 2:4-7*
3. **Presented with gifts;** Psalm 72:10 & Isaiah 60:6; *Matt. 2:1,11*
4. **Herod will kill children;** Jeremiah 31:15; *Matt. 2:16-18*

III. HIS SPIRITUAL NATURE (DIVINE)

1. **His pre-existence;** Micah 5:2 & Isaiah 9:6-7 & Prov. 8:22-23; *John 1:1-2, 8:58, 17:5,24 & Col. 1:17 & Rev 1:17*
2. **He shall be called LORD;** Psalm 110:1; *Matt. 22:43-45 & Luke2:11*

IV. HIS MINISTRY

1. **He will crush the head of Satan;** Gen. 3:15; *Heb. 2:14 & 1 John 3:8*
2. **He will be a Prophet;** Deut. 18:18; *Matt. 21:11 & John 6:14*
3. **He will be a Priest;** Psalm 110:4; *Heb. 3:1, 5:5-6, 7:26-27*
4. **He will be a Judge;** Isaiah 11:4, 33:22; *John 5:30 & 2 Tim. 4:1*
5. **He will be a King;** Psalm 2:6 & Zech.9:9 & Jer. 23:5; *Matt. 27:37, 21:5 & John 18:33-38*
6. **He will have a special anointing of the Holy Spirit;** Isaiah 11:2, 42:1, 61:1-2; *Matt. 3:16-17, 12:17-21 & Luke 4:15-21,43 & John 1:32*
7. **His zeal for God will be great;** Psalm 69:9; *John 2:15-17*
8. **He will be preceded by a messenger;** Isaiah 40:3 & Malachi 3:1; *Matt. 3:1-3, 11:10 & Luke 1:17 & John 1:23*
9. **His ministry will begin in Galilee;** Isaiah 9:1; *Matt. 4:12-13,17*
10. **His ministry will be one of miracles;** Isaiah 35:5-6, 32:3-4; *Matt. 9:32-35, 11:4-6 & Mark 7:32-35 & John 5:5-9, 9:6-11, 11:43,44,47*

11. He will teach in parables; Psalm 78:2; *Matt. 13:34-35*

12. He will enter into the temple; Malachi 3:1; *Matt. 21:12*

13. He will enter Jerusalem on a donkey; Zech. 9:9; *Matt. 21:6-11 & Luke 19:35-37*

14. He will be a stumbling block to the Jews; Psalm 118:22 & Isaiah 8:14, 28:16; *1 Peter 2:7 & Romans 9:32-33*

15. He will be a light to the nations; Isaiah 49:6, 60:3; *Acts 13:47-48, 26:23, 28:28 & Luke 2:30-32*

V. GOOD FRIDAY

1. He will be betrayed by a friend; Psalm 41:9, 33:12-14; *Matt, 10:4, 26:49-50 & John 13:21*

2. He will be sold for 30 pieces of silver; Zech. 11:12-13; *Matt.26:15, 27:3-7*

3. He will be forsaken by his disciples; Zech. 13:7; *Matt 26:31 & Mark 14:27,50*

4. He will be silent before his accusers; Isaiah 53:7; *Matt 27:12-14 & Luke 23:9 & 1 Peter 2:22-25*

5. He will be wounded and bruised; Isaiah 50:6, 53:5 & Zech. 13:6; *Matt. 26:67, 27:26 & 1 Peter 2:24*

6. He will be mocked; Psalm 22:7-8, 69:8-13; *Matt. 27:29-31,39*

7. His hands and feet will be pierced; Psalm 22:16 & Zech. 12:10; *Luke 23:33 & John 20:25*

8. He will be crucified with thieves; Isaiah 53:12; *Matt. 27:38 & Mark 15:27-28 & Luke 22:37*

9. He will pray for those who persecute Him; Isaiah 53:12; *Luke 23:34*

10. He will be hated without a cause; Psalm 69:4; *John 15:25*

11. His garments will be parted and cast for lots; Psalm 22:18; *John 19:23-24*

12. He will suffer thirst; Psalm 69:21; *John 19:28*

13. He will give a forsaken cry; Psalm 22:1; *Matt. 27:46*

14. He will commit himself to God; Psalm 31:5; *Luke 23:46*

15. His bones will not be broken; Exodus 12:46 & Psalm 34:20; *John 19:33,36*

16. **There will be darkness over the land;** Amos 8:9; *Matt. 27:45*
17. **He will be buried in a rich man's tomb;** Isaiah 53:9: *Matt. 27:57-60*

APPENDIX B

Sharing the Doctrine of the Trinity
"... there is no God but one ..." 1 Corinthians 8:4

Prov. 30:4, Gen. 1:26, Isaiah 6:8, 9:5, Matt. 28:19, John 10:30, 14:9,11, 2 Cor. 13:13

I. ATTRIBUTES OF GOD:

FATHER
SON
HOLY SPIRIT

EVERYONE IN THE TRINITY IS DESCRIBED AS FOLLOWS:

1. Eternal
Rom. 16:26
Rev. 22:13
Heb. 9:14

2. Holy
Rev. 4:8
Rev. 15:4
Eph 4:30
Act 3:14
Acts 5:3

3. Truth
John 7:28
Rev. 3:7
John 14:6
John 14:17
1 John 5:7

4. Omnipresent
Jer. 23:24
Matt. 28:20
Psalm 139:7
Gen. 1:2

5. Omnipotent
Gen. 17:1
Rev. 1:8
Luke 1:35
Rev. 15:3
Acts 1:8

6. Omniscient
Isaiah 46:9–10
John 21:17
1 Cor. 2:10
Acts 15:18
Isaiah 40:13, 14

7. Creator
Genesis 1:1
Col. 1:16
Job 33:4
John 1:3

II. FUNCTIONS OF GOD:

FATHER
SON
HOLY SPIRIT

EVERYONE IN THE TRINITY IS INVOLVED IN THE FOLLOWING:

1. Giving us eternal life
Rom. 6:23
John 10:25,28
Gal. 6:8

2. Salvation
Titus 3:4–5
Matt. 1:21
2 Thess. 2:13

3. Resurrection of Jesus
Acts 2:32
John 2:19–20
1 Peter 3:18

4. Inspiration of Prophets
Heb. 1:1–2
2 Cor. 13:3
Mark 13:11

5. Comforting us
2 Thess. 2:16-17:
2 Thess. 2:16-17
John 15:26

6. Baptism
Matt. 28:19
Matt. 28:19
Matt 28:19

III. ALL THREE PERSONS OF THE TRINITY MENTIONED IN THE SAME VERSE:

Isaiah 48:16, 61:1, 2 Cor. 13:14, Matt. 28:19, Gal. 4:6, John 15:26, 1 Tim. 3:16, Acts 2:33, 1 Thess. 3:13, Rom. 8:9, Heb. 9:14, 1 Cor. 12:3

Recommended Resources and Reading
The resources in this list will help you better understand and share with Muslims.

For additional reprints of this booklet or more in-depth study, please order:
• *ISLAM 101* by Lorraine Orris
• *The JESUS Film* (Available in Arabic, French, Farsi, Pashto, and other Muslim-world languages)
• *Handbook of Today's Religions,* by Josh McDowell 0-8407-3501-4
• *Craig vs. Ally* Videos, by William Craig 1942V-CI

Available from your local Christian bookstore or call:
Toll Free: (800) 827-2788, M—F 9am—6pm EST,
or 24/7 go to: www.campuscrusade.org

ADDITIONAL SUGGESTED READINGS

• Read at least part of the Qur'an (up to about surah 6, at minimum). Note: Many Muslims will not accept your ability to reference the Qur'an unless you have read it in Arabic. Never mind the fact that many Muslims cannot read and understand it themselves. If you are serious, learn Arabic. Even if you cannot do that, read it in English. You can also get a good English/Arabic version and have them explain to you how they interpret the passages in question. Don't debate; let the Spirit convict them.

• *Answering Islam: The Crescent in the Light of the Cross.* Norman L. Geisler and Abdul Saleeb (Grand Rapids, MI: Baker Books, 1998). A serious and scholarly examination of Muslim claims; a Christian evaluation from a logical, scholarly standpoint, and a Christian rebuttal. Saleeb (not his real name) is a former Muslim and on several government "hit lists." Absolutely essential reading.

- *The Qur'an and the Bible in the Light of History and Science,* Dr. William Campbell (available as a zip file from answering-islam.org at http://zipfiles.answering-islam.org/campbell_bq.zip)

- *Islam Revealed: A Christian Arab's View of Islam,* Dr. Anis Shorrosh, (Nashville: Thomas Nelson Pub., 1988).

- *Miniskirts, Mothers, and Muslims,* Christine Mallouhi

- *Jesus Among Other Gods,* Ravi Zacharias & Kevin Johnson, (Nashville: Word Pub., 2000).

- *Light in the Shadow of Jihad, Ravi Zacharias,* (Sisters, OR: Multnomah Pub., 2002).

- www.Answering-Islam.org - What it sounds like. Contains many articles, a comprehensive index to Islamic and Qur'anic names and terms, and numerous downloadable books.

- http://www.the-good-way.org/ - A page targeted at ministering directly to Muslims. Contains an Arabic Bible online and a few links to apologetics pages.

- http://www.injil.com/ - Contains apologetics tools for reaching Muslims.

- http://db.islam.org:81/Quran/ssearch.htm - The Qur'an on-line, searchable.

- http://www.islam101.com/ - Information on Islam from a Muslim perspective.